Challenge of Space written by: Robin Kerrod
Illustrated by: Derek Bunce, Jeff Burn, Wilfred Hardy,
            John Harwood, John Marshall, Mike Roffe
Cover illustrated by: John Marshall

Mission Outer Space written by: Robin Kerrod
Illustrated by Derek Bunce, Andrew Farmer, John Harwood,
            John Kelly, John Marshall, Lee Noel, Geoff Taylor,
            Ian West

Designed by: Tri-Art
Series Editor: Christopher Tunney
Art Director: Keith Groom

Published by Christensen Press Limited, The Grange,
Grange Yard, London SE1 3AG.
© Christensen Press Limited 1985

First published 1985
Revised edition 1990

Printed and bound by Graficas Reunidas, Madrid, Spain.

ISBN: 0 946994 09 9

THE CHALLENGE OF
Space

Φ   Christensen Press

What is space?

SPACE We live in one of the most exciting periods of history. Today we can do something people have been dreaming about for centuries—we can travel in space. Men started going into space in 1961, only four years after the first man-made moon was launched. Now they can fly hundreds of thousands of kilometres across space to the real Moon. Yet at the beginning of this century nobody had succeeded in flying an aeroplane even a few hundred metres!

The Earth we live on has around it a thin layer of gases, which we call the *atmosphere*. Near the ground the atmosphere is quite thick. But it gets thinner the higher we rise above the Earth's surface. Above about 160 km (100 miles), there is hardly any atmosphere left. Then we are in space.

Where is the Earth in space?

Sun

Mars

White dwarf star

Red giant star

Moon

The Earth is one of a multitude of bodies that exist in space. Between these bodies there is nothing except a few atoms of gas and specks of dust. Earth is a planet, which travels with eight others around the Sun. The Sun is a star—the nearest star to us. Like most other stars, it is a ball of glowing gas.

How big is space?

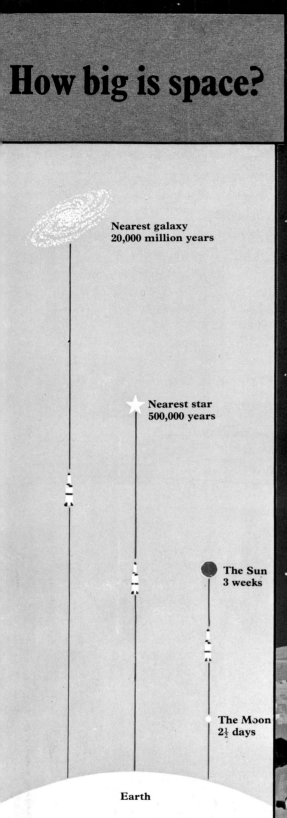

Nearest galaxy
20,000 million years

Nearest star
500,000 years

The Sun
3 weeks

The Moon
2½ days

Earth

It is difficult to imagine how big space is. But an idea of its size can be gained if we imagine setting out to explore it in a rocket. In our rocket, we would reach the Moon in about 2½ days, and the Sun in about 3 weeks. But it would take us over half a million years to reach even the next nearest star, and thousands of millions of years to reach the nearest galaxy.

What is it like in space?

Up in space, there is no air. So there can be no sound, because sound needs air to travel in. There can be no clouds, no rain, no snow. Space is dark. You can see things only when sunlight shines on them. In the Sun, it is very hot. Out of the Sun, it is deathly cold.

Why go into space?

Space, then, is a hostile world for Man. And travelling in space is very dangerous. So why go there? One of the main reasons is that it presents a challenge to Man's inventive mind. It is there, waiting to be explored. And by exploring space, Man finds out more about how the universe is made up and how we fit into it.

The Challenge of Space 1

GETTING INTO SPACE When men decided to explore space, they had to find means of getting there. Many difficulties had to be faced and overcome. The main problem to be solved was how to defeat the pull of the Earth, which attracts every object to its surface. When men found a way of overcoming this pull, they were able to launch a body into space, to become an artificial moon of the Earth.

What is gravity?

We call the pull of the Earth *gravity*. Because of gravity, everything we throw or drop falls to the ground. And every falling object accelerates towards the Earth at the same rate. This means that light objects fall as quickly as heavy ones.

How does gravity affect us?

Gravity affects things profoundly. It keeps our feet firmly on the ground. It keeps the atmosphere in place. All the heavenly bodies have gravity too. It is the Moon's gravity that attracts the water in the oceans and causes the tides. The Sun's powerful gravity keeps the planets (including the Earth) circling around it in space. The bigger a body is, the greater is its gravity.

Who first thought of gravity?

The first person to realize that gravity is a basic force of the universe was Isaac Newton, one of history's most brilliant thinkers. It is said that he thought out his ideas on gravity after seeing apples fall from a tree in his garden.

How can we beat gravity?

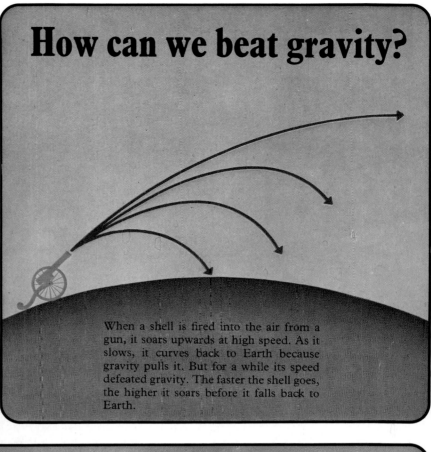

When a shell is fired into the air from a gun, it soars upwards at high speed. As it slows, it curves back to Earth because gravity pulls it. But for a while its speed defeated gravity. The faster the shell goes, the higher it soars before it falls back to Earth.

What is a satellite?

If you had a very powerful gun indeed, you could fire the shell so fast that it would overcome gravity and stay up in space. To do so, it must travel at more than about 28,000 kph (17,500 mph). At this speed, it can circle around the Earth as an artificial moon, or *satellite*.

Flight path of satellite

Satellite climbs into orbit

Why does it not fall down?

A satellite stays in its orbit (path) around the Earth for a long time, because there is no air or anything else to slow it down. But if it does slow down, gravity will pull it back to Earth.

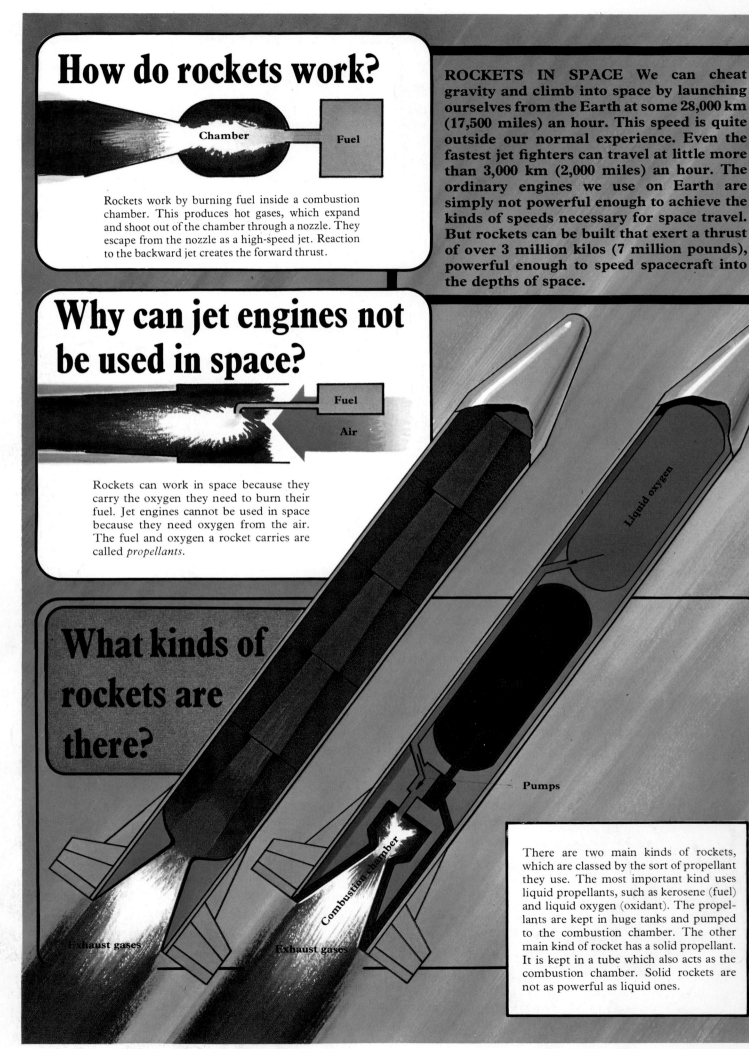

How do rockets work?

Rockets work by burning fuel inside a combustion chamber. This produces hot gases, which expand and shoot out of the chamber through a nozzle. They escape from the nozzle as a high-speed jet. Reaction to the backward jet creates the forward thrust.

Chamber

Fuel

Why can jet engines not be used in space?

Rockets can work in space because they carry the oxygen they need to burn their fuel. Jet engines cannot be used in space because they need oxygen from the air. The fuel and oxygen a rocket carries are called *propellants*.

Fuel

Air

What kinds of rockets are there?

ROCKETS IN SPACE We can cheat gravity and climb into space by launching ourselves from the Earth at some 28,000 km (17,500 miles) an hour. This speed is quite outside our normal experience. Even the fastest jet fighters can travel at little more than 3,000 km (2,000 miles) an hour. The ordinary engines we use on Earth are simply not powerful enough to achieve the kinds of speeds necessary for space travel. But rockets can be built that exert a thrust of over 3 million kilos (7 million pounds), powerful enough to speed spacecraft into the depths of space.

Liquid oxygen

Pumps

Combustion chamber

Exhaust gases

Exhaust gases

There are two main kinds of rockets, which are classed by the sort of propellant they use. The most important kind uses liquid propellants, such as kerosene (fuel) and liquid oxygen (oxidant). The propellants are kept in huge tanks and pumped to the combustion chamber. The other main kind of rocket has a solid propellant. It is kept in a tube which also acts as the combustion chamber. Solid rockets are not as powerful as liquid ones.

What is a step rocket?

No single rocket is powerful enough to lift itself into orbit. A space launcher must be made up of several rockets, one on top of the other. This arrangement is called a *step rocket*. Each rocket fires in turn, dropping away when its fuel is spent. As a result, the launcher becomes progressively lighter and faster as it climbs into space.

How big are rockets?

Space rockets are huge. Even the smallest stand 30–40 metres (100–130 feet) high. The biggest are real skyscrapers! The most massive rocket to date has been the mighty Saturn V rocket that launched the Apollo spacecraft on their epic journeys to the Moon. It stood no less than 111 metres (365 feet) high on the launch pad.

The Photon Rocket

Present-day rockets can travel very fast, but scientists have suggested ways of making rockets that will travel many times faster still. One design would use an intense beam of light as a propellant. It is known as the *photon* rocket.

Why are satellites useful?

MAN-MADE SATELLITES The launching of the first two sputniks by Russia in 1957 signalled the beginning of the Space Age. Twenty years later there were more than 4,000 bits and pieces of man-made 'hardware' circling the Earth in space. They included satellites that were working, satellites that had ceased to work, and parts of the rockets that had launched them. All the man-made objects in space circle at different heights. The lower ones will eventually slow down and fall back into the atmosphere, where they will burn up like shooting stars.

Satellites are very useful, particularly to scientists studying the Earth and the heavenly bodies. They are valuable for studying the Earth because they can view all its surface within a few days or weeks. Satellites are useful in astronomy because they are above the Earth's distorting atmosphere.

What shape are they?

Molniya

IUE

OTS

Exosat

Intelsat

Geos

Satellites can be any shape. They do not have to be streamlined like bodies that travel through the air, because there is no air in space. So they can be made any shape that is convenient for the job they have to do.

What are they like inside?

Early satellites used ordinary batteries to provide electricity for their instruments. But most modern satellites use solar cells. These cells are made of wafers of silicon. These produce electricity when sunlight falls on them.

Scientific instrument

Guidance unit

Upper platform

Satellites differ inside, depending on their purpose. But they are all made up of several units that perform different functions. There will, for example, be an instrument unit, which will carry a variety of instruments, a power unit, and a communications unit.

Solar cells (power unit)

Upper body structure

Cooling system

Main platform (includes communication and control units)

How do we keep track of them?

Propellant tanks

Rocket motor

Space scientists keep track of satellites by means of radio and radar. They listen in to radio beams the satellites transmit, or bounce radio beams off them (radar), using large dish aerials.

SATELLITES AT WORK Satellites have already proved themselves very useful for many purposes, and their use will grow in the years ahead. They have, for example, brought about a revolution in communications. They have made it possible to transmit live television programmes between countries on opposite sides of the world. Satellites have also helped weathermen to improve their forecasting, and astronomers to see the universe more clearly.

What do weather satellites tell us?

How do communications satellites work?

Communications satellites contain powerful amplifiers. They receive a radio beam from one ground station, strengthen it, and then beam it back down to another. Many are in stationary orbits 35,900 km (22,300 miles) above the Earth. From Earth, they appear to be fixed in the sky.

Weather satellites are equipped with cameras to take pictures of the cloud formations in the atmosphere. They also carry instruments to sense what conditions are like there. As they circle around the Earth, they provide information about the global weather scene, which makes weather forecasting much easier.

Have astronomy satellites made any discoveries?

Can satellites be used for mapping?

Astronomy satellites have made some very interesting discoveries. They have discovered peculiar X-ray stars, for example, that give off their energy in short, rapid bursts. They have found evidence of mysterious bodies called *black holes* that swallow up all matter.

Satellites have proved very useful in cartography (map-making). Photographs taken from space show the Earth's surface very clearly, and enable maps to be made with great accuracy. Using high magnification, even city streets can be made out. Ocean currents and depths are also often visible.

What else can they be used for?

The photographs and images taken by satellites provide information about rock formations, vegetation, water resources, and many other things. Satellites can also act as radio beacons for navigation and as platforms to collect information.

How do people live in a satellite?

Air freshening units

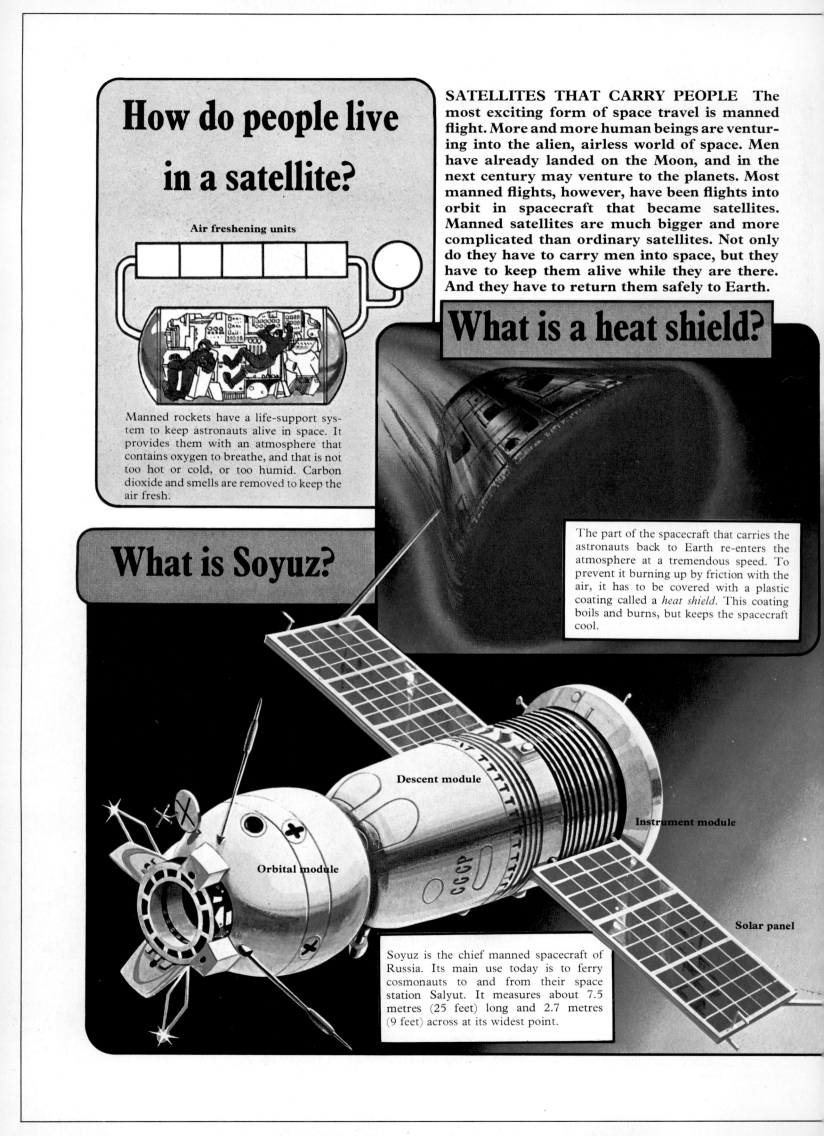

Manned rockets have a life-support system to keep astronauts alive in space. It provides them with an atmosphere that contains oxygen to breathe, and that is not too hot or cold, or too humid. Carbon dioxide and smells are removed to keep the air fresh.

SATELLITES THAT CARRY PEOPLE The most exciting form of space travel is manned flight. More and more human beings are venturing into the alien, airless world of space. Men have already landed on the Moon, and in the next century may venture to the planets. Most manned flights, however, have been flights into orbit in spacecraft that became satellites. Manned satellites are much bigger and more complicated than ordinary satellites. Not only do they have to carry men into space, but they have to keep them alive while they are there. And they have to return them safely to Earth.

What is a heat shield?

The part of the spacecraft that carries the astronauts back to Earth re-enters the atmosphere at a tremendous speed. To prevent it burning up by friction with the air, it has to be covered with a plastic coating called a *heat shield*. This coating boils and burns, but keeps the spacecraft cool.

What is Soyuz?

Orbital module

Descent module

Instrument module

Solar panel

Soyuz is the chief manned spacecraft of Russia. Its main use today is to ferry cosmonauts to and from their space station Salyut. It measures about 7.5 metres (25 feet) long and 2.7 metres (9 feet) across at its widest point.

What was Apollo?

Command module

Service module

Rocket motor

Apollo was the spacecraft American astronauts used to travel to the Moon between 1969 and 1972. It had a length of about 10 metres (33 feet), and a maximum diameter of 3.9 metres (13 feet). Apollo spacecraft were also used for Skylab missions.

What is a module?

Like ordinary satellites, manned spacecraft are built up of a number of units, or *modules*. One is the crew or command module, which carries the astronauts. Another is the service or equipment module, which carries such things as fuel, power, and communications equipment, and rocket motors. Only the crew module returns to Earth.

Soyuz descent module

What is the control room like?

MISSION CONTROL Manned space launchings have been taking place since 1961, but all aspects of space travel are still very dangerous. Every space launching is the result of many months of detailed planning by a large team of scientists and engineers. During the actual space flight, a team of men at mission control are responsible for the successful operation of the launching rocket and the spacecraft. They are also responsible for the safety of the men who are being carried into space.

Who is in charge?

In overall charge of the flight is the flight director. He keeps an eye on all the many different aspects of the mission, and also receives reports from other specialists. He makes all the decisions that affect flight operations.

This view of the Houston control centre became familiar to television viewers during the Apollo Moon missions. Groups of controllers sit at control desks, or *consoles*, and follow every stage of the flight. They watch instruments and television screens linked by radio with the distant spacecraft.

Who are the other main controllers?

One controller is in continuous voice contact with the astronauts in the spacecraft. He is usually an astronaut himself, and knows exactly what it is like in space. The Americans call him *Capcon*.

Another controller watches the flight path of the spacecraft to ensure that it is accurate. The exact position of the craft must always be known, otherwise the mission becomes very dangerous indeed.

A third controller keeps a check on the mass of data (information) that comes from the many systems in the spacecraft. It tells him whether the systems are operating as they should.

What goes on behind the scenes?

Where are the U.S. tracking stations?

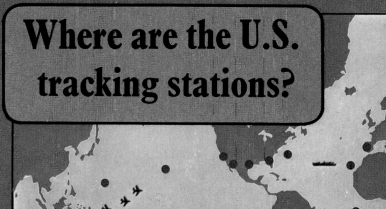

The people sitting at the consoles in the mission control centre are really the 'tip of the iceberg'. They are in contact with other experts who advise them on problems they can't deal with. These experts can be shown any of the pictures or data mission control receives.

America's Spaceflight Tracking and Data Network (STDN) provides the vital link between mission control and the astronauts. It has stations spaced around the Earth to ensure continuous communication.

What is weightlessness?

LIVING IN ORBIT (1) Travelling in space is a strange experience for human beings, who are used to living with their feet planted firmly on the ground by gravity. But in orbit there is no gravity. This creates peculiar problems, as we shall see. Up in space, astronauts and cosmonauts have to work very hard, keeping themselves and their spacecraft fit, and carrying out various experiments. And, always, at the back of their minds lurks the fear that something could go wrong—for they are in an alien world.

In orbit, objects do not have any weight, because there is no effective gravity. Everything is 'falling around the Earth' in the same way. This condition is known as *weightlessness*. It enables astronauts to float around and perform incredible feats of gymnastics.

What problems does it cause?

But weightlessness does cause problems. You cannot walk because there is nothing to keep your feet on the floor. Nothing stays where you put it. You cannot sit down to an ordinary meal at a table, because chairs, table, plates, and food just float away! There is no 'up' nor 'down' in space.

How do astronauts:

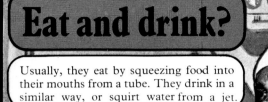

Eat and drink?

Usually, they eat by squeezing food into their mouths from a tube. They drink in a similar way, or squirt water from a jet.

Wash?

Washing in the ordinary way would send drops of water everywhere. So astronauts usually rub themselves down with wet towels. If they use a shower, it must be fitted with a vacuum device to suck up the drops.

Sit?

Because of weightlessness, chairs or stools have to be fixed to the 'floor' of the space-craft. The astronauts have to grip them with their legs, and slip their feet into straps to prevent themselves floating away.

Sleep?

Ordinary beds are of no use in space. They, the bed clothes, and the occupants would just float off. Astronauts therefore sleep zipped up in sleeping bags attached to their spacecraft.

What are the main parts of the shuttle?

The shuttle consists of three main parts. The crew live and work in the *orbiter*, a craft that looks much like a modern delta-winged jet airliner. This rides into space on a huge *tank*, which carries its fuel. Twin *booster rockets* are attached to the tank at take-off.

THE SPACE SHUTTLE

THE SPACE SHUTTLE Before 1981, all space launchings were made using huge step rockets. Since then, most American space launches have been made with a new type of spacecraft – the space shuttle. It is given this name because it shuttles back and forth between Earth and space. Unlike the step rocket, which can be used only once, the shuttle can be used time and time again. This makes space launchings much cheaper. The shuttle is also big enough to carry larger crews into space than was possible before.

Booster rocket

Orbiter

Main fuel tank

UNITED STATES OF AMERICA

Booster rocket

USA

What is special about the shuttle?

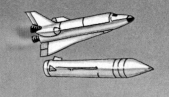

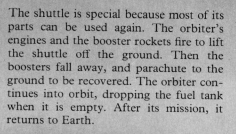

The shuttle is special because most of its parts can be used again. The orbiter's engines and the booster rockets fire to lift the shuttle off the ground. Then the boosters fall away, and parachute to the ground to be recovered. The orbiter continues into orbit, dropping the fuel tank when it is empty. After its mission, it returns to Earth.

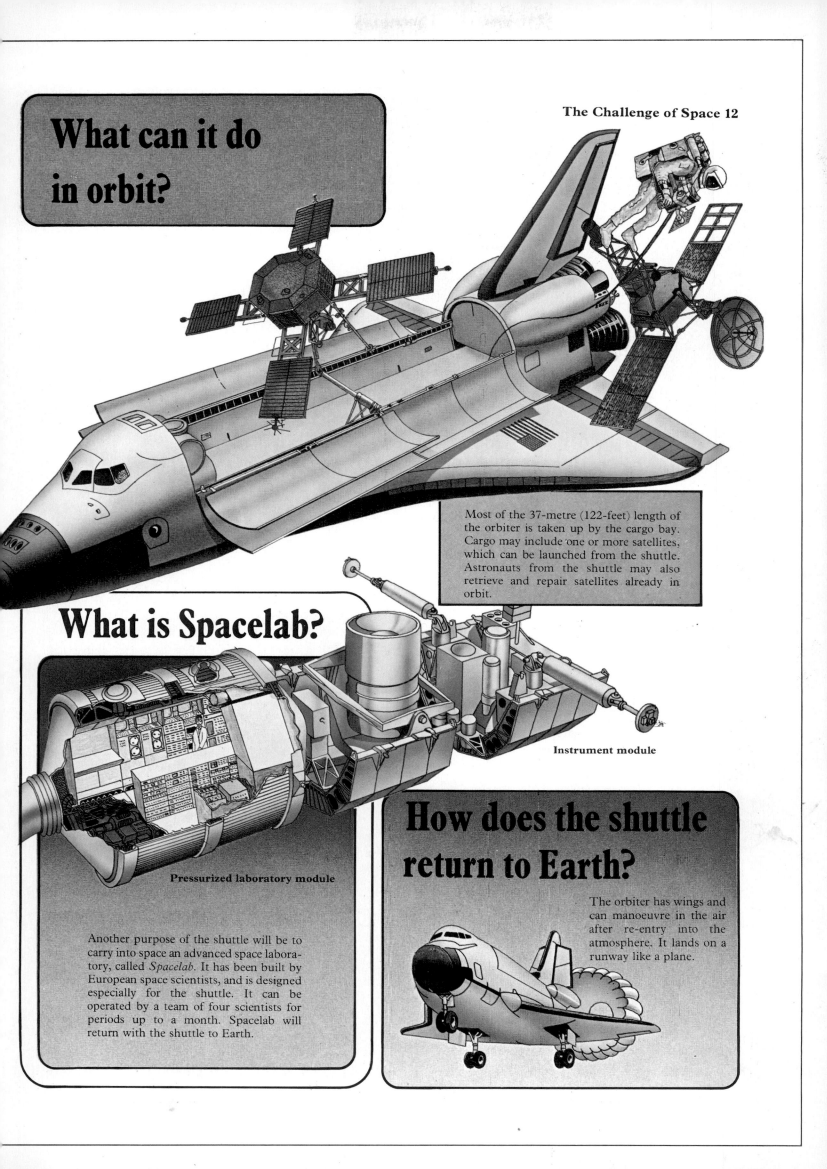

What can it do in orbit?

Most of the 37-metre (122-feet) length of the orbiter is taken up by the cargo bay. Cargo may include one or more satellites, which can be launched from the shuttle. Astronauts from the shuttle may also retrieve and repair satellites already in orbit.

What is Spacelab?

Instrument module

Pressurized laboratory module

Another purpose of the shuttle will be to carry into space an advanced space laboratory, called *Spacelab*. It has been built by European space scientists, and is designed especially for the shuttle. It can be operated by a team of four scientists for periods up to a month. Spacelab will return with the shuttle to Earth.

How does the shuttle return to Earth?

The orbiter has wings and can manoeuvre in the air after re-entry into the atmosphere. It lands on a runway like a plane.

What was Skylab?

SPACE STATIONS Ordinary manned spacecraft do not stay in space for long periods. They are not big enough to give the astronauts comfortable living space, or to carry sufficient provisions. For long missions, much larger space stations are required. By the end of the century, very large ones will be built. They will be permanently manned by scientists. Experimental space stations, such as the American Skylab and the Russian Salyut, have already paved the way.

Solar telescopes

Solar cells

Skylab was a space station built up from Apollo rocket parts. It was launched in 1973, and was visited over a period of eight months by three three-man teams of astronauts. They were ferried to it by Apollo spacecraft. The main part of Skylab was a large cylinder, which housed the crew. The whole cluster measured 36 metres (118 feet) long.

Solar cells

Orbital workshop

What was it like inside Skylab?

This picture shows the main living quarters in Skylab, taken by a rotating camera. They consisted of the wardroom, where the crew ate and relaxed; a toilet compartment; a sleep compartment; and an experiment compartment. Note the mesh floor.

Soyuz

**Soyuz about to dock
with Salyut**

Salyut

What is Salyut?

Salyut is a Russian space station design. By the late 1980s, seven Salyut stations had been launched into orbit, and visited by teams of cosmonauts for up to 212 days. Much smaller than Skylab, Salyut measures only about 12 metres (40 feet) long and some 4 metres (13 feet) across.

What will future space stations look like?

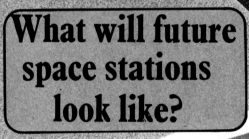

In the future, space stations will be much bigger than either Salyut or Skylab. They will probably be built up of large cylinders joined together. They may look like this. The side units will probably be laboratories devoted to various sciences, such as biology and physics.

How will they be built?

The separate sections of tomorrow's space stations will be ferried into orbit by space shuttles or larger craft. In orbit, the sections will be joined together by teams of skilled space engineers.

Steps into Space

Early science-fiction writers proposed other methods of travelling through space. The French writer Jules Verne imagined this 'moon train', which was designed to be fired from a huge cannon. Note the smoke coming from the chimney!

While some dreamed, others worked. In the United States, Robert Goddard experimented with a novel form of rocket—propelled not with solid gunpowder but with liquid petrol. In 1926, his first liquid rocket travelled 56 metres (184 feet).

The most important step in the history of space travel was the invention of the rocket. This followed the invention of gunpowder, the first rocket propellant, in about AD 900. Both inventions were made by the Chinese. The Chinese may have been using rockets in warfare at least as early as 1232.

Meanwhile, in Russia, in 1903, Konstantin Tsiolkovsky had laid down many of the principles on which space flight depends. He saw that rockets were the only means of propulsion in space, and that step rockets would be needed to get there. We call him 'the father of astronautics'.

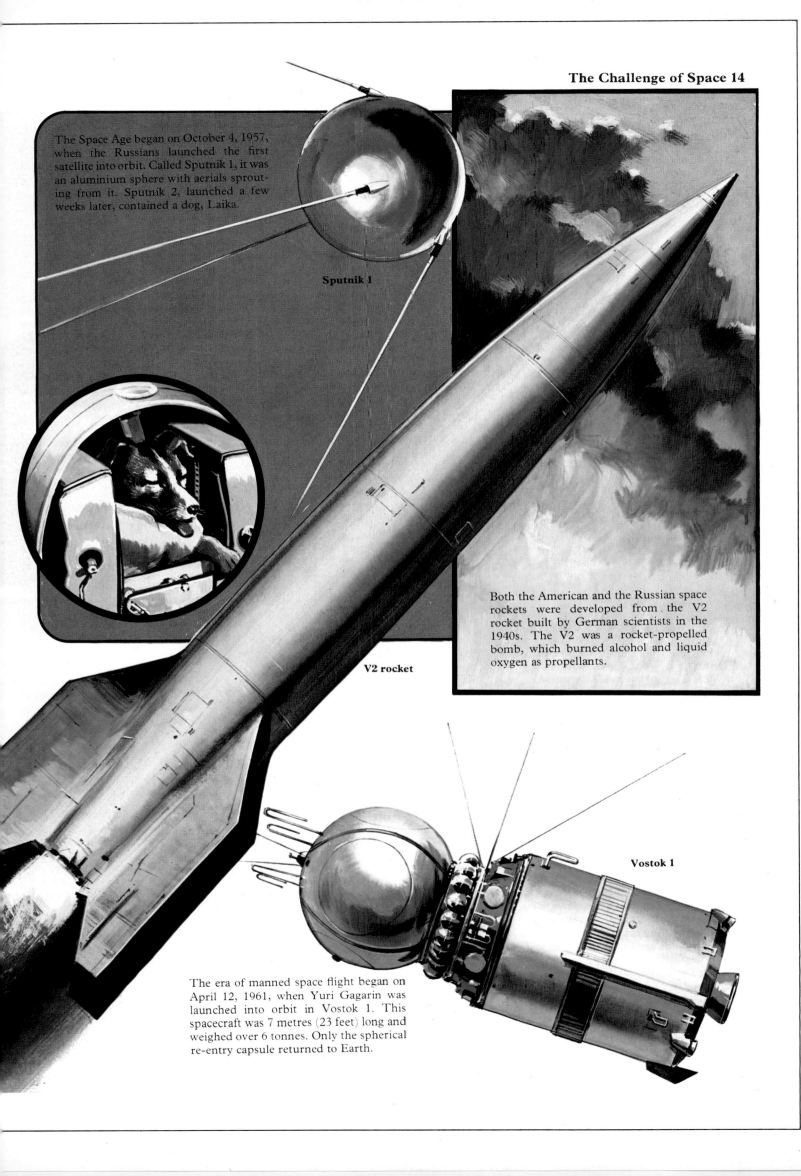

The Space Age began on October 4, 1957, when the Russians launched the first satellite into orbit. Called Sputnik 1, it was an aluminium sphere with aerials sprouting from it. Sputnik 2, launched a few weeks later, contained a dog, Laika.

Sputnik 1

Both the American and the Russian space rockets were developed from the V2 rocket built by German scientists in the 1940s. The V2 was a rocket-propelled bomb, which burned alcohol and liquid oxygen as propellants.

V2 rocket

Vostok 1

The era of manned space flight began on April 12, 1961, when Yuri Gagarin was launched into orbit in Vostok 1. This spacecraft was 7 metres (23 feet) long and weighed over 6 tonnes. Only the spherical re-entry capsule returned to Earth.

Famous Rockets and Satellites

Apollo American manned spacecraft. Housing a three-man crew, Apollo took astronauts to the Moon. The first Moon landing (Apollo 11) took place on July 20, 1969. The first manned flight (in orbit) took place on October 11, 1968. Apollo was also used to ferry astronauts to and from the Skylab space station in 1973–74, and in the first international space link-up with a Russian Soyuz crew, in 1975.

Ariel Scientific satellites designed by British space engineers and launched by the United States.

Atlas American rockets used to launch Mercury spacecraft. They burned kerosene and liquid oxygen as propellants.

Cosmos Russian scientific satellites.

Echo A huge balloon which was launched as the first communications satellite, in 1960.

ERTS Stands for Earth Resources Technology Satellite. The first was launched in 1972. Now renamed Landsat.

Explorer American scientific satellites. The first one was America's first satellite (launched January 31, 1958). It made the first scientific discovery of the Space Age—of the powerful belts of radiation we now call the Van Allen belts.

Gemini American two-manned spacecraft, named after the zodiacal constellation Gemini, the Twins. The first manned Gemini flight (Gemini 3) took place on March 23, 1965. There were nine in all.

Intelsat International communications satellites. Intelsat IV and IVa satellites relay television and telephone signals

between the continents from stationary orbits over the Atlantic, Pacific, and Indian Oceans.

Landsat Formerly ERTS. Earth survey satellites that photograph the Earth from space. Their photographs reveal a great deal about the Earth's resources and land mass.

Mercury American one-man spacecraft. Mercury 3 performed a manned orbital flight on May 5, 1961. John Glenn in Mercury 6 (called Friendship 7) became the first American in orbit on May 24, 1962.

Meteor Russian weather satellites.

Molniya Russian communications satellites.

Nimbus American weather satellites.

OAO Stands for Orbiting Astronomical Observatory. OAO Copernicus is famous as the first to detect the presence of a black hole.

Orbita The Russian satellite communications network.

Saturn American rockets used in their Apollo Moon landing project. Saturn V, the biggest rocket ever, stood 111 metres (365 feet) high and had three stages. Its take-off thrust was some 3 million kilos (7 million pounds).

Soyuz The main Russian manned spacecraft. It first flew on April 23, 1967. That flight resulted in the death of its cosmonaut, Vladimir Komarov, when the landing parachute failed. In 1978 two Soyuz craft docked with Salyut 6 space station to make the first ever triple space link-up.

Space shuttle American manned spacecraft, in operation since 1981. It is equipped with

booster rockets to propel it into space, and wings to enable it to return and land like an aircraft.

Sputnik Russian word for *satellite*. But most people think of Sputnik as the first Earth-orbiting satellite (October 4, 1957). It remained in orbit for 92 days. The second Sputnik, launched on November 2 of the same year, contained the first space traveller, a dog named *Laika*.

Telstar The first active communications satellite, which went into orbit in 1961.

Titan Launching rocket for America's Gemini flights. A two-stage vehicle, it had nitrogen tetroxide and Aerozine as propellants for both stages.

V2 Rocket bombs developed by the Germans in World War II. Called *Vergeltungswaffe zwei* (vengeance weapon two), it was first successfully tested in 1942, at Peenemünde in the Baltic, and used in the war in 1944.

Voshkod Early Russian manned spacecraft. The word means *sunrise*. Voshkod 1 was the first craft to take three men into space together, on October 12, 1964. Cosmonaut Aleksei Leonov in Voshkod 2 (March 18, 1965) became the first man to walk in space.

Vostok The first Russian manned spacecraft. Yuri Gagarin became the first man in orbit on April 12, 1961, in Vostok 1. *Vostok* means *east*. Six Vostok flights took place in all, the last on June 16, 1963. This carried the first woman into space—Valentina Tereshkova.

MISSION OuterSpace

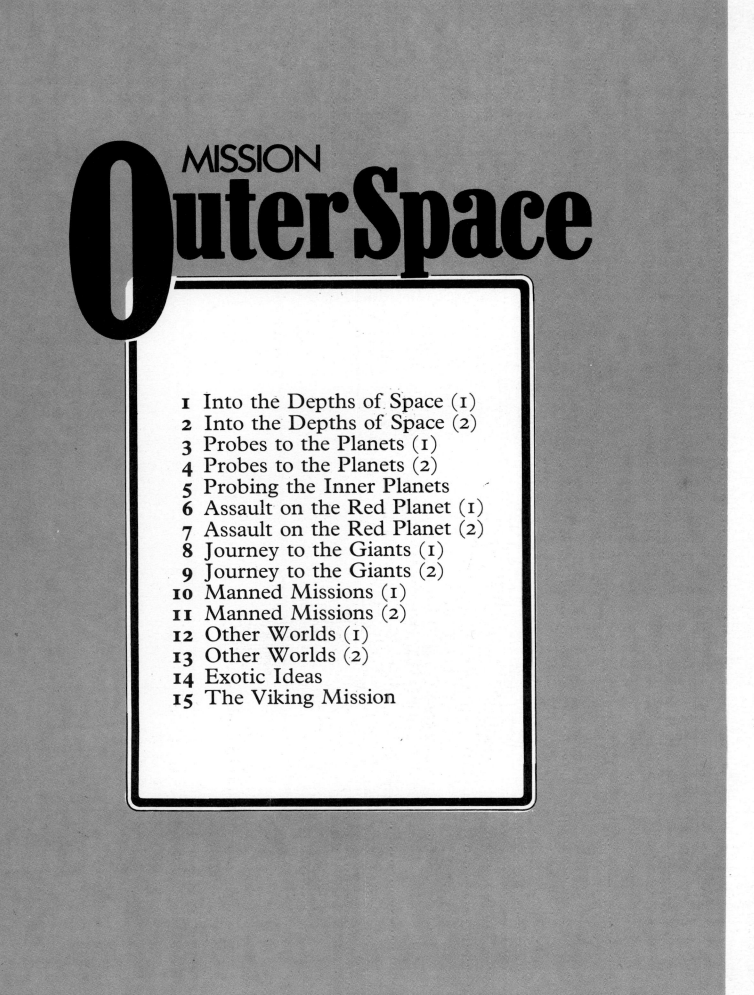

Why are the planets worth studying?

INTO THE DEPTHS OF SPACE (1) Hundreds upon hundreds of spacecraft have been launched into orbit and to the Moon since the Space Age began. They have sent back a wealth of information about the Earth, the Moon, and the space in which they float. Other spacecraft have been sent to probe the mysteries of deeper space, wherein lie the wandering planets, asteroids, and comets.

Giant Jupiter is by far the largest planet in the solar system.

Saturn is the most distinctive body in the heavens

Mars has long been regarded as the planet most likely to support life.

Venus shines brilliantly as the evening star.

Mercury looks much like the Moon.

Men have been studying the planets since the beginning of civilization. They have always been fascinated by the way the planets wander through the heavens. By finding out more about them, we hope to get a better idea of the structure of the universe and our place in it.

How do we study them?

We can study the motion of the planets with just our eyes, like the ancients did. And with telescopes we can pick out a few details of their surface. But only by sending spacecraft, or probes, to them can we find out what they are really like. The probes may go into orbit around the planet or even land on it.

Mission Outer Space 1

Will man ever reach the planets?

Men have already reached the Moon. But launching men to the planets would be very much more difficult and dangerous. Much more powerful rockets would be required, and even then a round trip would take many months rather than a few days. But almost certainly one day men *will* make the trip.

What lies beyond the solar system?

The farthest planet in the solar system, Pluto, lies over 5,000 million km (3,000 million miles) from the Sun. Some comets lie even farther away. Beyond them stretch vast regions of space that are empty except for traces of gas here and there. Then, many millions of millions of kilometres farther on lie other stars.

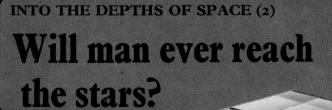

Will man ever reach the stars?

The stars lie so far away across the depths of space that it seems most unlikely that Man will ever be able to reach them. Even if he had a rocket as fast as light itself (which is not possible), a round trip to the nearest star would take nearly 10 years.

What lies beyond the stars?

Though stars are so very far apart, they are in fact clustered into a great star system, or galaxy. The stars in the sky all belong to the Milky Way galaxy. Beyond the Milky Way, across regions of empty space, lie other galaxies.

Mission Outer Space 2

The Size of the Universe

The planets and their stars; the stars and their galaxies; and all of space make up what we call the universe. No one knows where the universe begins and ends, or indeed *if* it begins or ends. We cannot therefore really say how big the universe is. All we can say is how big is the universe that we can observe. Through their most powerful telescopes, astronomers can detect objects in the heavens so far away that their light takes up to 15,000 million years to reach us. We say these objects lie up to 15,000 million light-years away. In terms of kilometres this would be 15 followed by 22 noughts (9×10^{22} miles)!

Will the universe ever end?

The universe appears to have existed for at least 15,000 million years. Astronomers have been trying to discover how much longer it will last. Some believe that it will never end, but just go on for ever. Others think that all the galaxies, which appear to be rushing away from each other, will one day start to come together again. When they meet, the present universe will end.

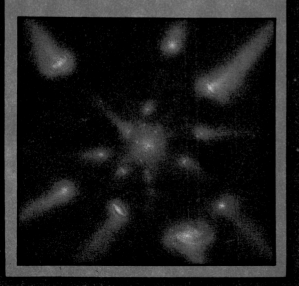

What shape is the universe?

Just as the size of the universe is unknown, so is its shape. We tend to think of the universe as being a sphere, because that is how it appears to us. But this might be an illusion. Some of the different shapes the universe could be are shown above, depending on whether starlight travels in straight lines or in positive or negative curves.

How do probes reach the inner planets?

Probes must travel in a very precise path to reach their target. To reach the inner planets, they must be launched against the direction that Earth is travelling in its orbit. Then they will eventually end up travelling slower than Earth. This means that the Sun will pull them closer—that is, in towards the orbits of the inner planets.

1	Venus
2	Sun
3	Mercury
4	Earth
5	Moon

... and the outer planets?

When a probe is destined for a planet farther from the Sun than Earth, it must be launched *in* the direction the Earth is travelling in its orbit. Then it eventually ends up travelling faster than Earth. This means that it will spiral away from the Sun—that is, towards the outer planets.

1	Earth
2	Moon
3	Sun
4	Mars
5	Jupiter
6	Saturn

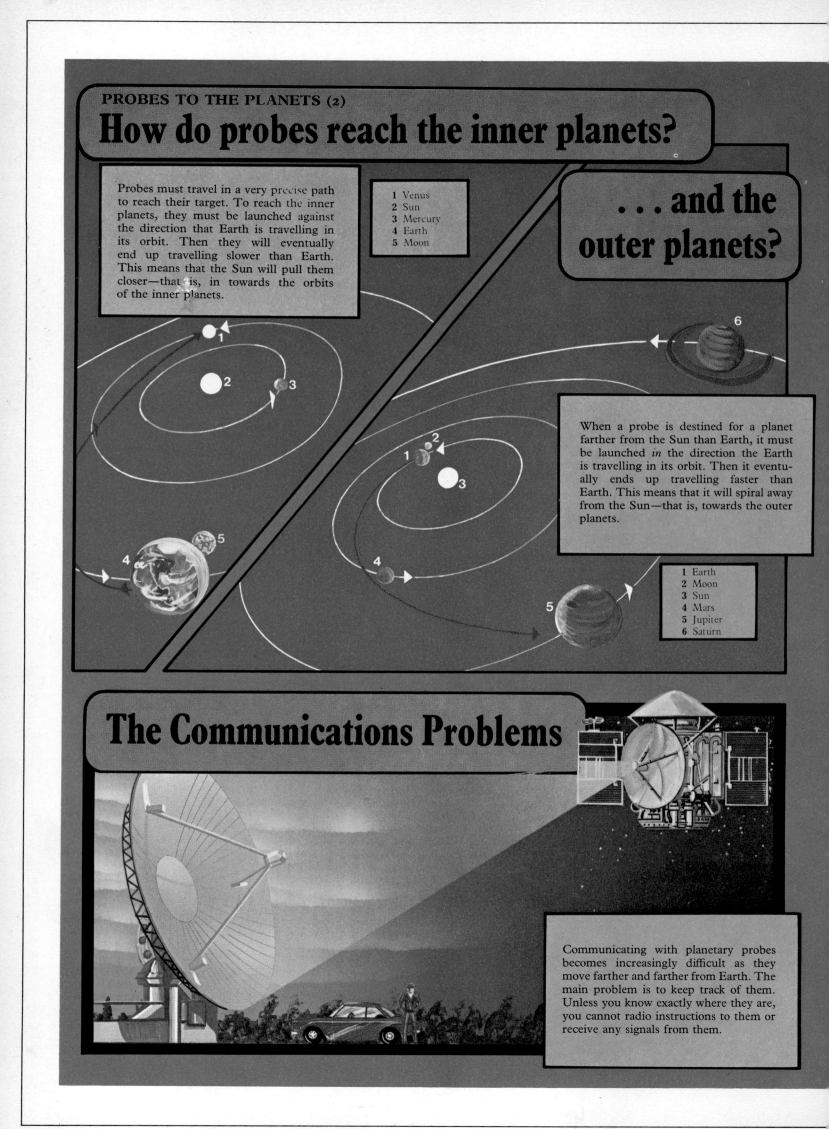

The Communications Problems

Communicating with planetary probes becomes increasingly difficult as they move farther and farther from Earth. The main problem is to keep track of them. Unless you know exactly where they are, you cannot radio instructions to them or receive any signals from them.

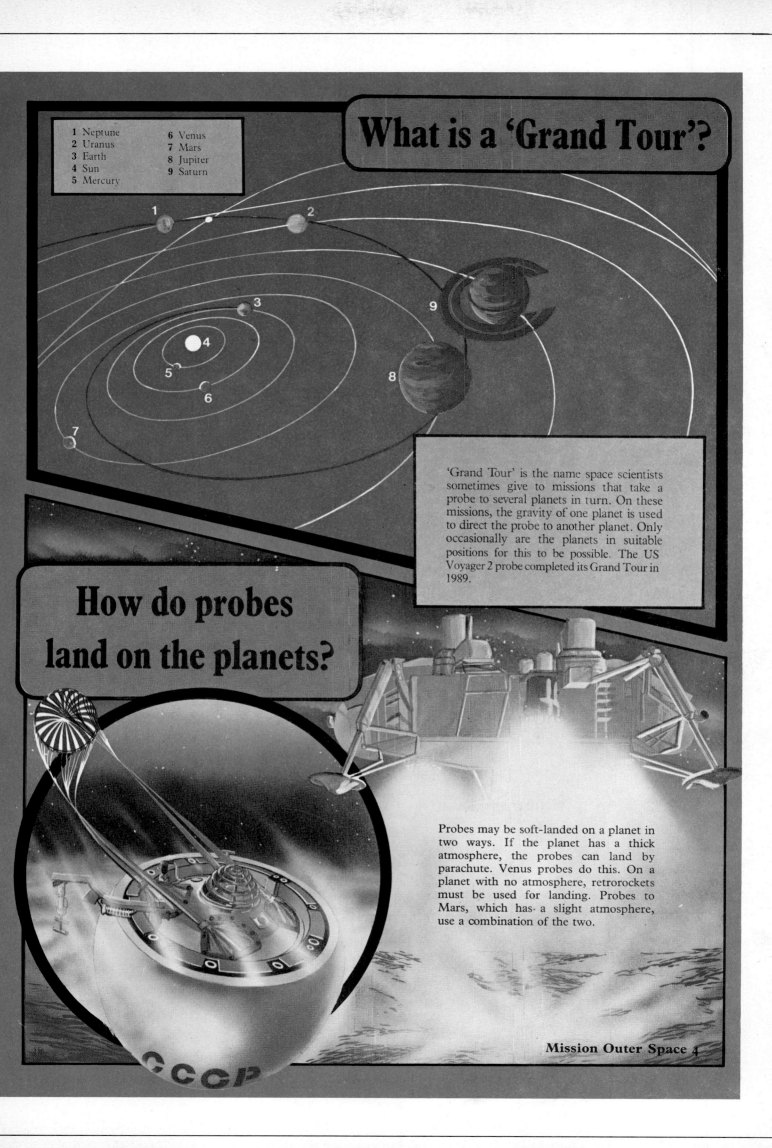

1 Neptune
2 Uranus
3 Earth
4 Sun
5 Mercury
6 Venus
7 Mars
8 Jupiter
9 Saturn

What is a 'Grand Tour'?

'Grand Tour' is the name space scientists sometimes give to missions that take a probe to several planets in turn. On these missions, the gravity of one planet is used to direct the probe to another planet. Only occasionally are the planets in suitable positions for this to be possible. The US Voyager 2 probe completed its Grand Tour in 1989.

How do probes land on the planets?

Probes may be soft-landed on a planet in two ways. If the planet has a thick atmosphere, the probes can land by parachute. Venus probes do this. On a planet with no atmosphere, retrorockets must be used for landing. Probes to Mars, which has a slight atmosphere, use a combination of the two.

Which probe first went to Mercury?

Mariner 10 was the first probe to visit Mercury and send back pictures of its surface. It was launched in November 1973, and passed by the planet three times between March 1974 and March 1975. At its closest approach it was only about 300 km (190 miles) above the surface.

PROBING THE INNER PLANETS The two planets that lie inside the Earth's orbit have intrigued astronomers for centuries. Small Mercury is so close to the Sun that it can be seen well only rarely, and no details of its surface are visible even in large telescopes. Venus, which is a near twin of the Earth in size, is always veiled in thick white clouds. They make the planet shine brighter than any object in the night sky except the Moon, but they hide its surface.

What did it discover?

The photographs Mariner 10 took of Mercury show the planet to be much like the Moon in appearance. The whole surface is covered with craters, but there are no large 'seas', or *maria*, as there are on the Moon. As was expected, there were no signs that Mercury has an atmosphere.

What else did it do?

Before Mariner 10 reached Mercury, it travelled to Venus. It then used the gravity of Venus to swing it in towards the orbit of Mercury. This gravity-assist method helps save power. Mariner 10 took some excellent pictures of Venus, showing bands of clouds swirling in the thick atmosphere.

What is Venus really like?

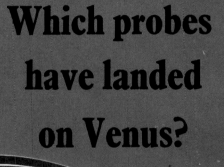

In reality, Venus has proved to be an enormous hothouse, with a thick, suffocating atmosphere of carbon dioxide. Temperatures soar to more than 400°C, and pressures are 100 times those on Earth. The surface is barren and strewn with rocks. No kind of life as we know it could survive under such conditions.

Which probes have landed on Venus?

Venus the Myth

Because of its closeness to the Earth and its similar size, people once reckoned that Venus might harbour life. They imagined that luxuriant vegetation grew there, in which giant reptiles like dinosaurs thrived.

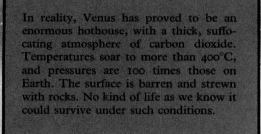

The Russians have sent several probes to Venus. These probes, called *Venera*, eject a capsule, which then parachutes down to the surface. The early Venera capsules were crushed or burned up in the atmosphere of Venus. But Venera 4 soft-landed on the planet in 1967, and later Veneras sent back pictures of the surface in 1975 and 1978.

Why is Mars so fascinating?

Mars is the only planet whose surface can be seen from Earth. Powerful telescopes reveal that the planet has polar ice caps, which come and go with the Martian seasons. They show dark surface markings, which also change shape from time to time. In the late 1800s, some astronomers reported that they could see straight markings like canals, which they reckoned could have been made by intelligent creatures.

ASSAULT ON THE RED PLANET (1) Mars is a much smaller planet than either Earth or Venus. But it approaches quite close to us—nearer than 56 million km (35 million miles) at times. And it is one of the most distinctive heavenly bodies because of its orange-red colour. Because of its fiery hue, the Romans named the planet after their god of war. Probes have now mapped the planet in detail.

Which spacecraft first went to Mars?

The US probe Mariner 4 made the first successful fly-by of the red planet in July 1965. It passed within 9,000 km (5,500 miles) of Mars and sent back several pictures that showed a cratered surface. It also reported traces of an atmosphere.

'The Martians Are Coming'

The reported discovery of 'canals' on Mars captured people's imagination. And they made up fanciful tales of a dying Martian race. The myth was fostered by H. G. Wells's masterly novel *The War of the Worlds* (1898), in which he described an invasion of Earth by Martian war machines. In 1938, Orson Welles produced a radio play based on the book in such a realistic way that thousands of Americans believed that Martians had landed and were devastating their country.

Which spacecraft became Mars's third moon?

Mars has only two satellites, or moons, called Phobos and Deimos. In November 1971 it gained a third moon—the US probe Mariner 9. It arrived in Martian orbit while the planet was gripped in a gigantic dust storm, which hid surface details. But when the storm cleared, the probe sent back beautifully clear pictures of the surface.

Has Russia launched any Mars probes?

Russian space scientists began launching probes to Mars before the Americans. But none of them has been very successful. Communications were lost with Mars 1 (1962/3) when success seemed near. In 1971/2, Russian probes joined Mariner 9 in orbit and released landing capsules. One managed to land safely, but survived only for a few seconds. It was probably destroyed in the violent dust storm that was then raging.

What kinds of things did Mariner 9 find?

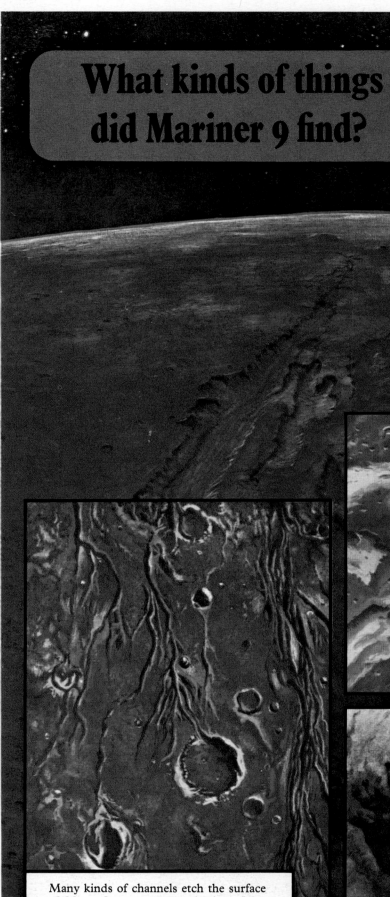

Many kinds of channels etch the surface of Mars. Some appear to be lava flows from ancient volcanoes. Some might even have been made by flowing water. Others are faults caused by movements of the Martian surface. The biggest is a deep rift valley, 5,000 km (3,000 miles) long and up to 65 km (40 miles) wide.

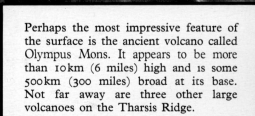

Perhaps the most impressive feature of the surface is the ancient volcano called Olympus Mons. It appears to be more than 10 km (6 miles) high and is some 500 km (300 miles) broad at its base. Not far away are three other large volcanoes on the Tharsis Ridge.

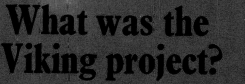

What was the Viking project?

Viking was a successful attempt to land US probes on Mars. In the summer of 1975, two Viking probes set off on a year-long journey that took them 800 million km (500 million miles) through space to Mars. They were made up of two parts: one remained in orbit, while the other descended to the surface.

What is the Martian surface like close up?

Both Viking probes landed successfully in different regions of Mars. But their views of the Martian surface were very similar. They showed a landscape of rocks scattered in sandy soil. The over-all colour was a dark orange. The sky was tinted a pale pink, probably because of the dust it contained.

JOURNEY TO THE GIANTS (1) Far beyond Mars lies the giant of the solar system—Jupiter. Unlike the planets nearer the Sun, Jupiter is made up mainly of gas. It has been said that if Jupiter had been a little bigger, it would have become a second Sun. The next three planets beyond Jupiter—Saturn, Uranus and Neptune—are also huge compared with the Earth. Even these planets, which lie thousands of millions of kilometres away, are now within range of our probes.

Rocket motor

Instrument package

Nuclear batteries

Dish antenna

Which spacecraft first went to Jupiter?

The American probe Pioneer 10 became the first probe to fly-by Jupiter in December 1973. The voyage to Jupiter took the 260-kg (570-lb) craft two years across a distance of 1,000 million km (620 million miles). It passed within 130,000 km (80,000 miles) of the planet, taking measurements and photographs.

Magnetometer

How was it powered?

Pioneer could not be powered by solar cells like some planetary probes, because the strength of sunlight near Jupiter is only a fraction of what it is near Earth. It was powered instead by nuclear batteries, which convert the heat given out by radioactive atoms into electricity.

What was its flight like?

Pioneer was boosted from Earth at a speed of nearly 52,000 kph (32,000 mph), which was then the fastest speed ever reached by a man-made object. This speed caused it to spiral outwards, across the orbit of Mars and through the asteroid belt. It arrived at Jupiter within one minute of the estimated time.

What information did it send back?

Pioneer's television cameras sent back a number of pictures of the planet, showing its cloud belts and the mysterious Red Spot. Instruments revealed that the planet is made up mainly of hydrogen. This exists as gas in the thick atmosphere and in liquid form underneath. Jupiter has a strong magnetic field and powerful radiation belts. It also gives off radiation, rather as the Sun does. Its Red Spot appears to be a huge storm.

What did it carry?

Besides the usual instruments and equipment, Pioneer 10 carried a gold plaque. On this plaque was drawn a message to any intelligent creature who might come across the probe, perhaps millions of years hence. It depicts a naked Earth man and woman, with an outline of the probe behind them to indicate scale. The other diagrams describe where in the solar system the Earth is, and where the solar system is located in space.

Where is Pioneer 10 now?

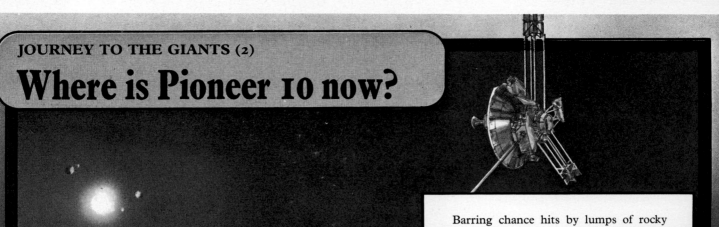

Barring chance hits by lumps of rocky matter, Pioneer 10 will survive indefinitely. By 1978 it was travelling in deep space in the vicinity of the orbit of Uranus. In 1983 it crossed the orbit of the then outermost planet, Neptune. It is now heading for the stars.

What was unusual about Pioneer 11's flight?

Exactly a year after Pioneer's encounter with Jupiter, a near-identical probe, Pioneer 11, was transmitting information about the planet back to Earth. But it approached much closer (41,000 km, 25,500 miles) and from a different direction. It looped around Jupiter in a corkscrew-like path that directed it towards Saturn, which it reached in 1979.

Why were scientists eager to get a close-up view of Saturn?

Saturn has a rare beauty, because of its system of glistening rings. They were photographed close-up, first by Pioneer II, but most magnificently by Voyager 1 and 2. They prove to be made up of hundreds of separate ringlets.

What other probes have been sent to the giant planets?

Two Voyager probes (1 and 2) visited Jupiter and Saturn in turn between 1979 and 1981. They sent back spectacular pictures of the planets and their moons. Voyager 2 then flew on to Uranus for a rendezvous in 1986, and Neptune in 1989.

What message is Voyager carrying?

Like the Pioneer probes, the Voyagers are carrying messages for beings who might find them in the future. They are in the form of a disc recording, which includes typical sounds and pictures of Earth in electronic form.

John Kelly

Will people travel deep into space?

MANNED MISSIONS (I) Man did not venture into space until 1961, yet less than 8 years later they set foot on the Moon. By now they are capable of remaining in space for periods of up to 8 months. It seems certain that in the years ahead they will undertake much longer voyages beyond the Moon to explore regions where only unmanned craft have so far been.

There are many problems to be solved before human beings venture beyond the Moon. One is to design a spacecraft powerful enough to cover vast distances in space quickly. Another is to provide life support for the crew on voyages that will last for a year or more.

What kind of spacecraft will they use?

Solar panels

Main spacecraft

Nuclear rockets

Present-day chemical rockets are not suitable for continuous operation for long periods, because they burn their fuel too fast. Space scientists think that nuclear rockets might be the answer. They would use the energy of nuclear reactors as a power source to accelerate a gas such as hydrogen into high-speed jets. The nuclear reactors would be sited far away from the crew quarters to prevent radiation damage.

How will they support themselves?

Space travellers would not be able to carry enough food, water, and oxygen for voyages lasting for a year or more. They would have to be self-supporting. They would grow plants in chemical solutions in greenhouse modules. They would recycle, or use again and again, liquid and solid wastes.

Where will they go first?

The Longest Space Flight

On October 2, 1984, three Russian cosmonauts returned triumphantly to Earth after setting a new space endurance record of 237 days in their orbiting space station Salyut 7. They were Leonid Kizim, Vladimir Solovyov and Oleg Atkov. During their record-breaking mission, the three cosmonauts were visited by two other three-person crews. The first, in April, included the first Indian to go into space, Rakesh Sharma. The second visiting crew, in July, included Svetlana Savitskaya, making her second trip into space. She made space history by becoming the first woman to make a spacewalk, carrying out cutting, welding and soldering operations on metals.

The first destination for deep-space travellers will be Mars, which is one of our planetary neighbours. Venus is somewhat nearer, but is too hot to visit. Mars is quite cold and has only a slight atmosphere, but people could explore it in spacesuits. When Earth and Mars are in favourable positions in space, a manned round trip to Mars could be completed in about 20 months.

Mission Outer Space 10

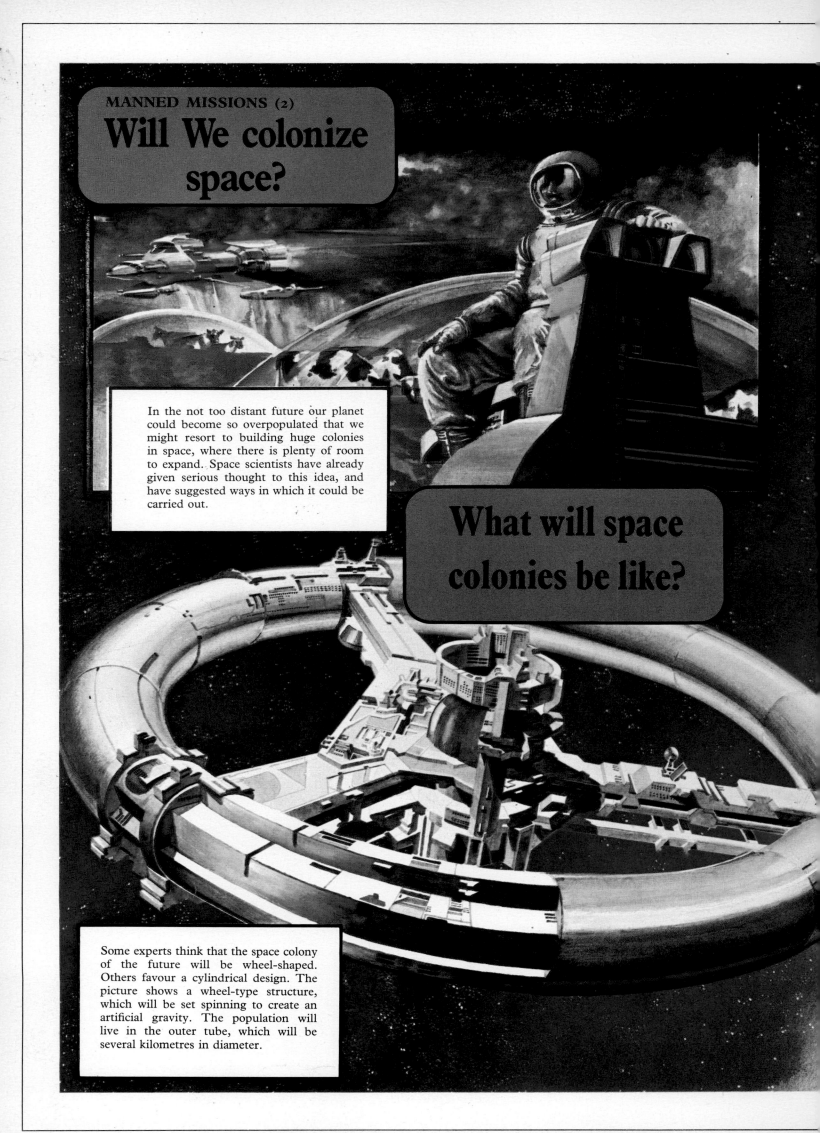

Will We colonize space?

In the not too distant future our planet could become so overpopulated that we might resort to building huge colonies in space, where there is plenty of room to expand. Space scientists have already given serious thought to this idea, and have suggested ways in which it could be carried out.

What will space colonies be like?

Some experts think that the space colony of the future will be wheel-shaped. Others favour a cylindrical design. The picture shows a wheel-type structure, which will be set spinning to create an artificial gravity. The population will live in the outer tube, which will be several kilometres in diameter.

What will they be like inside?

Inside the tube there will be houses, shops, and fields, rivers and lakes. They will be kept in place by the artificial gravity. The tube will be pressurized, and sunlight will be reflected into it by mirrors. Shutters will cut off the light for part of the time to imitate night. Electricity to power the colony will come from solar energy.

How will they be built?

Space colonies will take a long time to build. The engineering side will not be too difficult. The main problem will be ferrying the materials out into space. One day, metals to build the colonies may be smelted in space from ores mined on the Moon.

Are there planets around other suns?

OTHER WORLDS (1) One of the questions that Man has asked for centuries is: Is there life on other worlds? And if there is life, what will it be like? Some people report that they have seen 'flying saucers', which they believe come from another world. But so far there is no real evidence that beings or things from outer space have visited or tried to communicate with Earth.

We must rate the chances of there being solar systems similar to our own as very high indeed. The universe consists of millions of galaxies, each containing millions of stars much like the Sun. So even our galaxy must contain many stars with planetary systems. And astronomers have found some evidence that one or two of the nearest stars have planets circling around them.

Do they harbour life?

Until we receive messages or visits from beings of another planet, we have no way of telling if any of the planets circling around other stars harbour life. Again, we must argue that they do, unless we assume that conditions for life exist only on *this* planet, in *this* solar system, in *this* galaxy, in *this* part of the universe.

Sun

Life zone

Mercury **Too hot**

Earth

Venus

Mars

Too cold

The Zone of Life

There is around every star a region that provides the right temperature for life as we know it to exist. We call it the *zone of life*. In our solar system the only planet within this life zone is Earth. Venus lies a little too near the Sun and is too hot, while Mars lies too far away and is too cold. A planet in the life zone must also be a certain size for life to flourish, for it must be big enough to have an atmosphere.

How did life begin on Earth?

The way life began on Earth might also give us a clue to whether life exists elsewhere. Scientists think that the building blocks of life were formed when lightning and sunlight acted upon the early atmosphere, which contained gases such as ammonia and methane.

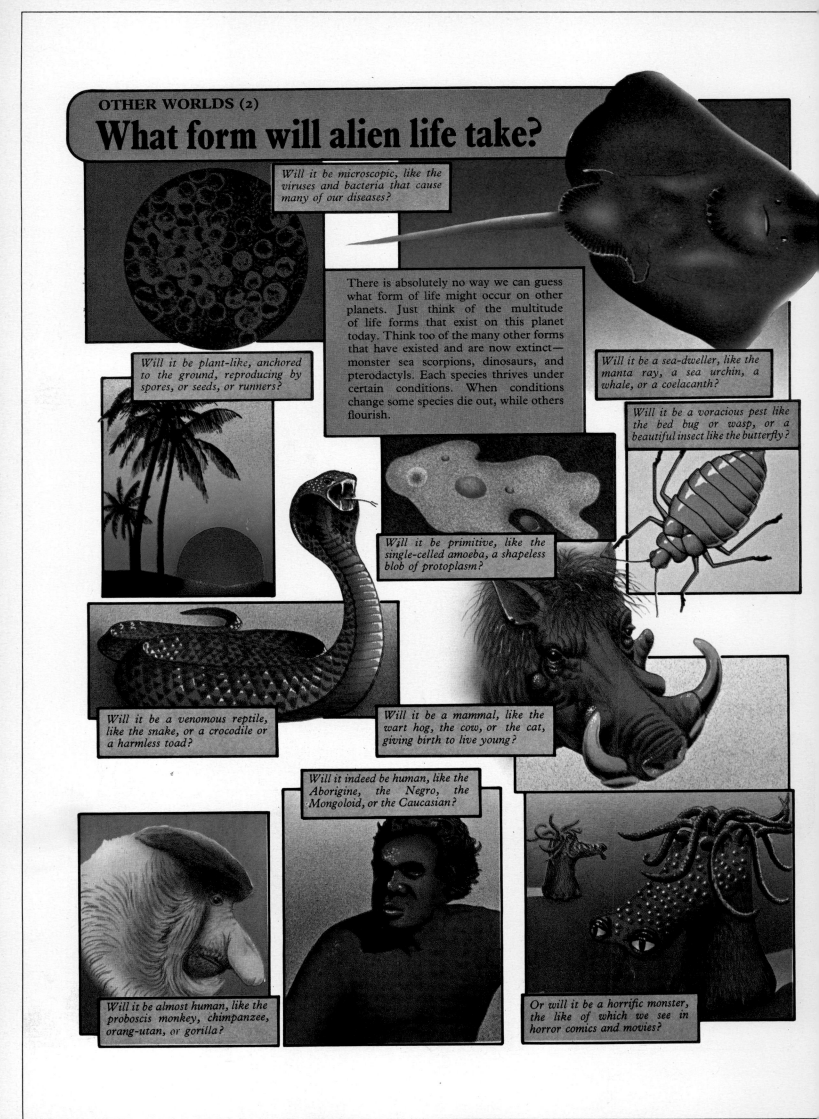

What form will alien life take?

Will it be microscopic, like the viruses and bacteria that cause many of our diseases?

There is absolutely no way we can guess what form of life might occur on other planets. Just think of the multitude of life forms that exist on this planet today. Think too of the many other forms that have existed and are now extinct— monster sea scorpions, dinosaurs, and pterodactyls. Each species thrives under certain conditions. When conditions change some species die out, while others flourish.

Will it be a sea-dweller, like the manta ray, a sea urchin, a whale, or a coelacanth?

Will it be plant-like, anchored to the ground, reproducing by spores, or seeds, or runners?

Will it be a voracious pest like the bed bug or wasp, or a beautiful insect like the butterfly?

Will it be primitive, like the single-celled amoeba, a shapeless blob of protoplasm?

Will it be a venomous reptile, like the snake, or a crocodile or a harmless toad?

Will it be a mammal, like the wart hog, the cow, or the cat, giving birth to live young?

Will it indeed be human, like the Aborigine, the Negro, the Mongoloid, or the Caucasian?

Will it be almost human, like the proboscis monkey, chimpanzee, orang-utan, or gorilla?

Or will it be a horrific monster, the like of which we see in horror comics and movies?

Are UFOs from another world?

Many people have reported seeing mysterious things flying about in the sky. Collectively they are called UFOs, or unidentified flying objects. The popular belief (or perhaps wish?) is that UFOs come from another world in outer space. But there is no evidence of this. They may merely be glimpses of man-made objects such as weather balloons or natural phenomena such as ball lightning

Could we communicate with other worlds?

We have the means of transmitting messages to and receiving them from other worlds in space in the giant radio telescopes astronomers now use. The problem is where to aim them. Unless they are pointing in the right direction, the signals would be lost. In addition, the distance to the stars is so great that there would be a time-lag of several years between sending a message and receiving a reply.

Beating Time

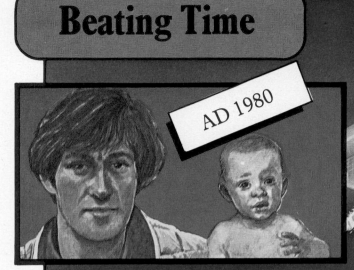

AD 1980

AD 2040

According to Einstein's theory of relativity, time passes more slowly the faster you travel. Suppose an astronaut aged 20 departs in 1980 on a trip to a distant star, leaving behind on Earth his new-born son. He travels at three-quarters the speed of light. When he returns to Earth in AD 2040, he finds that he is now the same age as his son.

Passage to a New Universe

Astronomers think that there are great voids, or *black holes*, throughout the universe, which suck everything into them, even light. The matter that is sucked in ceases to exist. Or does it? Some people have suggested that this matter reappears in another universe, through what they term a *white hole*. The holes are corridors between universes.

Colonizing Venus

The planet Venus is much like the Earth in size, but there the similarity ends. Venus is scorching hot, with a thick atmosphere of carbon dioxide. But some people have suggested that it could be changed into another Earth in time. First, primitive plants called algae would be injected into its atmosphere.

The algae would feed on the carbon dioxide and give off oxygen as they do so. Eventually the atmosphere would start to clear and lose heat. When it became cool enough, rain would fall and cool the land as it evaporated. This would happen again and again, the planet becoming cooler all the while.

One day, many centuries after the start of the project, the Sun would shine on Venus for the first time. Soon men from Earth would make their first landing. In no time at all a colony would be established, slowly converting the planet into a replica of Earth.

Building New Planets

An even more imaginative scheme has been suggested for the more distant future, when the nearby planets and the Moon have been colonized. New planets would be built within the life zone of the Sun. They would be constructed from the asteroids—the lumps of rock that orbit between Mars and Jupiter. The asteroids would be rocketed to a certain point in space, where gravity would fuse them into a solid mass.

The Grand Tours

On 25 August 1989, after a journey of 12 years across billions of kilometres of space, the Voyager 2 space probe swept past the planet Neptune just under 5000 kilometres from the planet's cloud tops. It sent back the first ever close-up pictures of this far-off world.

Voyager 2 lived up to all expectations, gathering valuable new information about this previously little-known planet. At each fly-by it took spectacular pictures that have revolutionized study of the planets and their moons.

Out to Saturn, Voyager 2 followed in the wake of its sister craft Voyager 1. But thereafter the two craft went their separate ways. Voyager 1 began heading out of the solar system, its most important work complete. Voyager 2, on the other hand, began heading for a rendezvous with the next planets out, Uranus and Neptune.

Gas Giants

The targets for the Voyager missions are the giants among the planets. Jupiter's diameter is over 11 times that of the Earth. Saturn's is nearly seven times as big. Unlike the Earth, though, Jupiter and Saturn are made up of gas, not rock. The other two large outer planets, Uranus and Neptune, are also globes of gas.

Before the Space Age began the giant planets held many mysteries. What was Jupiter's great Red Spot? What were Saturn's rings made of? What were the planets' moons like? Space probes have answered these questions and many more besides. The Pioneer 10 and 11 probes visited Jupiter first, and Pioneer 11 went on to Saturn. They greatly increased our knowledge of both planets, but they were no match for the two Voyagers. These 825-kg (1800-lb) craft carried much better instruments for probing the space environment. In particular they carried precision cameras which took highly detailed pictures. Between them, they sent back more than 50,000 pictures of the planets and their moons.

Into the Depths of Space

The Voyager probes started their epic voyages of discovery in 1977. Voyager 2 was in fact launched first, on August 20. Voyager 1 was launched on September 5. But it was boosted to a higher speed on a shorter trajectory (path). By the end of the year it had overtaken Voyager 2.

The launch vehicle for both craft was a Titan-Centaur three-stage rocket with two strap-on boosters. It stood about 50 metres (165ft) high on the launch pad. The launch site was Cape Canaveral in Florida.

The boosters and rocket stages fired in sequence, dropping away when they ran out of fuel. After just 10 minutes, Voyager, with the third-stage rocket still attached, entered a 'parking' orbit travelling at about 28,000 kph (17,500 mph). During the parking orbit, all Voyager systems were checked out and final computations were made to ensure that it would follow the correct trajectory to Jupiter. At exactly the right moment in the orbit, the third-stage rocket was re-ignited to boost the vehicle out of Earth orbit and into deep space at an Earth escape speed of over 40,000 kph (25,000 mph). Then the third stage separated, and a booster module on board Voyager fired to increase its speed still further.

The Long Coast

Voyager began speeding towards its distant target at over 11 kilometres (7 miles) a second. On command its various arms, or booms, unfolded into their working positions, and the craft looked as it does in the picture (right).

Next came critical manoeuvres to align the spacecraft so that its 3.7 metre (12 ft) dish antenna pointed Earthwards. This was essential so that radio signals could be transmitted and received between Earth control and Voyager over the vast distances of space during the months and years ahead.

To position itself accurately, the spacecraft was commanded to seek the Sun. The Sun-sensors look out through tiny windows set in the dish antenna. Thruster rockets on the craft fired to move it into the correct position. Then other thrusters fired to rotate the craft until its star-tracking sensors locked on to the bright star Canopus. Voyager was now in precisely the right attitude in space. It was just four hours after lift-off.

For months Voyager coasted silently towards its first target planet, Jupiter. For practically all of the time, it was unpowered. Only occasionally were its thrusters fired to adjust its speed so that it stayed exactly on course. Such adjustments are called trajectory correction manoeuvres.

Jupiter Encounter

Voyager 1 beat Voyager 2 to Jupiter by four months. It began scanning the giant planet with its TV cameras and 10 other instruments in January 1979. Two months later it was swooping down to within 280,000 km (173,000 miles) of the planet's surface. As it flew by, it was accelerated by Jupiter's enormous gravity and deflected into a path that would take it on to Saturn 20 months hence. This was an example of the gravity-assist method — using the gravity of one body to accelerate a probe to another.

Voyager 2 encountered Jupiter four months later, picking up where Voyager 1 had left off. Then it too swung round and headed for Saturn.

What astonishing things the Voyagers discovered at Jupiter: The planet has a faint ring system like Saturn. Its Red Spot is a gigantic hurricane that has been blowing for centuries. Winds howl through Jupiter's deep atmosphere at speeds of over 500 kph (300 mph). Lightning bolts flash through the atmosphere. On its large moon there are active volcanoes, which spew out sulphur 'lava' and make the moon a vivid yellow-orange colour.

Saturn Encounter

After months of hectic activity at Jupiter, Voyager's instruments shut down for the long cruise to Saturn. Not until August 1980 did Voyager 1 spring to life again and started observing the beautiful ringed planet. Its closest approach was in November, when it swooped to within 125,000 km (77,000 miles) of the cloud tops, travelling at a speed of 91,000 kph (57,000 mph). After its 2.2 billion-km (1.4 billion mile) journey, Voyager 1 was only 20 km (12 miles) off target!

The images sent back by Voyager 1, and by Voyager 2 nine months later, astonished even the project scientists at Voyager mission control at Jet Propulsion Laboratory, Pasadena, California. They showed that Saturn's three main rings are made up of hundreds upon hundreds of tiny ringlets. The ringlets are composed of lumps of ice and rock of various sizes and cannot be more than a few hundred metres thick. Another interesting find was that belts of wind course through Saturn's atmosphere at speeds of up to 1800 kph (1100 mph)!

The Voyagers also took the first close-up pictures of many of Saturn's moons. The largest moon, Titan, was seen to have a thick atmosphere — the only moon in the solar system to do so. The Voyagers also spied no less than 13 new moons, bringing the number of Saturn's moons up to 23! The smallest are only about 10 km (6 miles) across. Some of these moons act like 'shepherds' and keep the ring particles in orbit. Others seemingly play 'tag', alternately overtaking and then falling behind each other.

Uranus and Neptune

Voyager 2 used Saturn's gravity to swing into a trajectory that took it to Uranus in January 1986. The encounter was eagerly awaited because we could not see any details of the planet through even the largest telescope on Earth. Uranus was known to have five satellites, and that its axis was tipped at right-angles to those of other planets. In 1977, astronomers discovered that the planet was encircled by five rings: Voyager 2's cameras identified eleven rings. Also as a result of the space probe's fly-by, we now know that Uranus has (at least) fifteeen satellites.

Exciting discoveries were also made about Neptune, three and half years later. Voyager 2 revealed clouds and a very stormy and complicated weather pattern. It has a system of three faint rings, and eight moons, six more than previously identified. Spectacular pictures of Neptune's largest satellite, Triton,

were also sent back. These showed that it had an atmosphere, consisting mostly of nitrogen and methane. The surface, showing up in remarkable detail, has strange patterns of ridges and grooves, ice caps, and erupting volcanoes.

To the Stars

Where will the Voyagers go when their primary missions are over? In about 10 years time, travelling at a speed of some 60,000 kph (37,000 mph), they will escape from the solar system and head for the stars. They should still be able to send back information for some time afterwards.

Voyager 1 will head off in the direction of the star constellation we call Ursa Minor, or the Little Bear. Voyager 2 will make tracks for Canis Major, the Great Dog. In about 360,000 years it will pass relatively close to Sirius, the brightest star we see in the night sky.

Unless the Voyagers are struck by rocks or other space debris, they should survive for at least that long. Perhaps one day they might stray close to another planet in another star system and be found by intelligent beings there. Then, if those beings didn't know it before, they would realise that life exists elsewhere in the universe. Clues to the identity of the people who launched Voyager are contained on a copper record disc mounted on the craft.

Instructions on how to play the record are inscribed on the cover of the disc, in a (hopefully) recognizable code. The inscription also shows where in space Voyager came from. When they play the disc, the alien creatures will hear greetings from Earth in 60 languages and a message from one-time US President Jimmy Carter. There are also typical sounds of Earth of the natural and man-made world, from the haunting calls of whales to the roar of a rocket take-off. There is music from the world's greatest composers as well as pop music and folk songs. What a treat those aliens have in store!